Science Sight Word Readers ™

Whales and Dolphins

by Tracy Jones

ISBN 978-0-545-24793-1

Photographs © 2011: cover: Seapics.com/Masa Ushioda; back cover top: iStockphoto/Josh Friedman; back cover bottom: iStockphoto/Kristian Sekulic; page 1: iStockphoto/Olga Filatova; page 2: Seapics.com/Jonathan Bird; page 3 main: Seapics.com/Mike Johnson; page 3 inset: iStockphoto/Jon Patton; page 4: Seapics.com/Masa Ushioda; page 5: Seapics.com/Danny Frank; page 6 main: Seapics.com/Doug Perrine; page 6 inset: iStockphoto/syagci; page 7: Seapics.com/Masa Ushioda; page 8: Getty Images/Frederic Pacorel; page 9 main: Seapics.com/Joao Quaresma; page 9 inset: iStockphoto/Johan Swanepoel; page 10: Photo Researchers, NY/Art Wolfe; page 11: Seapics.com/Carlos Eyles; page 12 top: iStockphoto/Olga Filatova; page 12 bottom: Minden Pictures/Flip Nicklin; page 13: iStockphoto/Jan-Dirk Hansen; page 14: iStockphoto/Suzannah Skelton; page 15: iStockphotp/Josh Friedman; page 16 top: iStockphoto/Michel Lizarzaburu; page 16 bottom: iStockphoto/Alexey Tkachenko.

Photo research by Jenna Addesso; Design by Holly Grundon

12 11 10 9 8 7 6 5 4 3 2 1   11 12 13 14 15 16/0

Printed in the U.S.A.   40

First printing, March 2011

SCHOLASTIC INC.

NEW YORK • TORONTO • LONDON • AUCKLAND
SYDNEY • MEXICO CITY • NEW DELHI • HONG KONG

sperm whale

Fast Fact

Whales are mammals, the same **as** people.

Can you **believe** the **size of** whales?
They are the largest animals in the sea

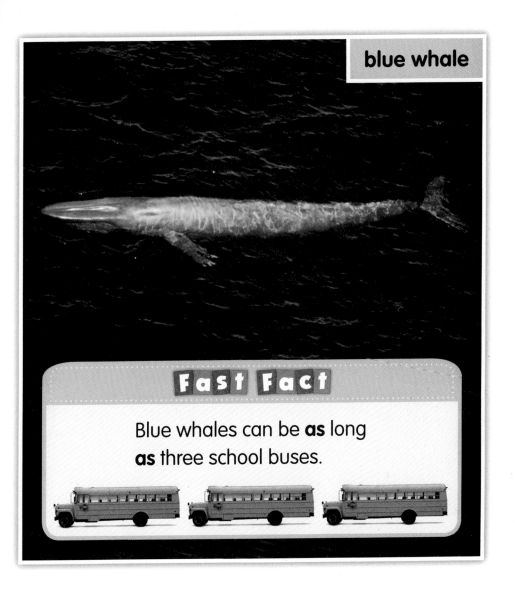

blue whale

Fast Fact

Blue whales can be **as** long **as** three school buses.

In fact, they are the largest animals on earth.

humpback whale

Fast Fact

It's called "breaching" when whales leap out **of** the water.

Can you **believe** the **size of** whales?
They make huge splashes.

gray whale

Fast Fact

Whales breathe air, just **as** people do.

They blow water high into the air.

Bryde's whale

Fast Fact

This whale can swallow thousands **of** little fish in one gulp.

Can you **believe** the **size of** whales? They eat lots **of** food.

humpback whale

Fast Fact

Humpback whales swim more than 6,000 miles per year.

They swim very long distances.

bottlenose dolphin

Fast Fact

Dolphins are mammals, the same **as** whales and people.

Can you **believe** the energy **of** dolphins? They frolic in the water.

striped dolphin

Fast Fact

Dolphins can leap 20 feet. That is **as** high **as** a giraffe.

They jump high into the air.

common dolphin

Squeak!

Fast Fact

Dolphins make noises such **as** clicks, squeaks, and whistles.

Can you **believe** the energy **of** dolphins? They make lots **of** sounds.

Atlantic spotted dolphins

Fast Fact

As many **as** 15 dolphins can live in one group.

They live together in groups.

beluga whale

spinner dolphin

Can you **believe** the **size of** whales and the energy **of** dolphins?

humpback whale

Fast Fact

It's called "lobtailing" when whales slap their tails against the surface of the water.

These two mammals are **as** amazing **as** can be!

Sight Word Review

Point to each sight word. Then read it aloud.

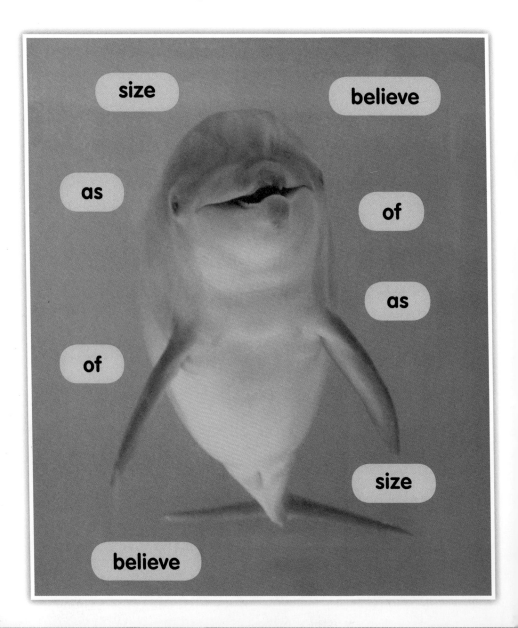

Sight Word Fill-ins

Use one sight word from the box to finish each sentence.

as	believe
of	size

❶ Look at the _____ of that whale!

❷ There are 45 different kinds _____ dolphins.

❸ It's hard to _____ that a blue whale is the length of three buses, but it's true.

❹ Dolphins are mammals, just _____ people are.

All About Whales and Dolphins

Ask a grown-up to read this with you.

Whales and dolphins are mammals. Even though they live in the ocean, they breathe air just like other mammals, so they have to come to the surface often. They breathe through blowholes on top of their heads. Just like other mammals, whales and dolphins also nurse their young with milk. Baby whales and dolphins are called calves.

humpback whale

bottlenose dolphin

Sometimes whales jump completely out of the water and come down with a huge splash. This is called breaching. No one is sure why whales do this. Maybe it's a way of communicating with other whales. Or maybe they are just having fun.

Dolphins are playful animals. In the wild, they play with seaweed as a toy. Dolphins live together in groups called pods. They communicate with each other in lots of different ways. They breach and lobtail just like whales. Each dolphin also has its own whistle. That way the dolphins in a pod can identify one another.